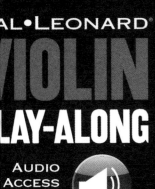

HAL•LEONARD® VIOLIN PLAY-ALONG

AUDIO ACCESS INCLUDED

PLAYBACK+
Speed • Pitch • Balance • Loop

To access audio visit:
www.halleonard.com/mylibrary
Enter Code
7671-8777-6553-8440

ISBN 978-1-4950-2993-6

7777 W. BLUEMOUND RD. P.O. BOX 13819 MILWAUKEE, WI 53213

Visit Hal Leonard Online at
www.halleonard.com

Jerry Loughney, violin
Audio arrangements by Dan Maske

Casey's Jig

Words and Music by Terry Casey

David's Jig

By Natalie MacMaster

7

Fisherman's Blues

Words and Music by Stephen Wickham and Mike Scott

I'm Shipping Up to Boston

Words and Music by Alexander Barr, Ken Casey, Woody Guthrie and Matthew Kelly

An Irish Party in Third Class

from the Paramount and Twentieth Century Fox Original Motion Picture Soundtrack BACK TO TITANIC

Words and Music by Samantha Hunt, Shep Lonsdale, Patrick Murphy,
Stephen Twigger and Stephen Wehmeyer

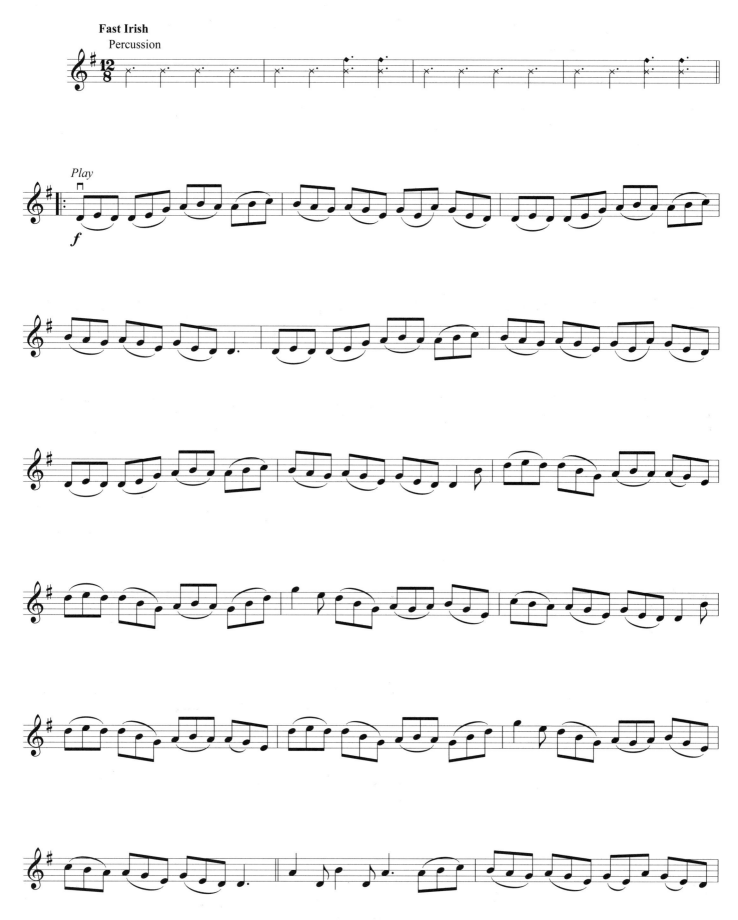

15

Lancaster Gate

**Words and Music by Trevor Lewington, Craig Downie,
Mark Abraham, James Campbell, Brian Buchowski**

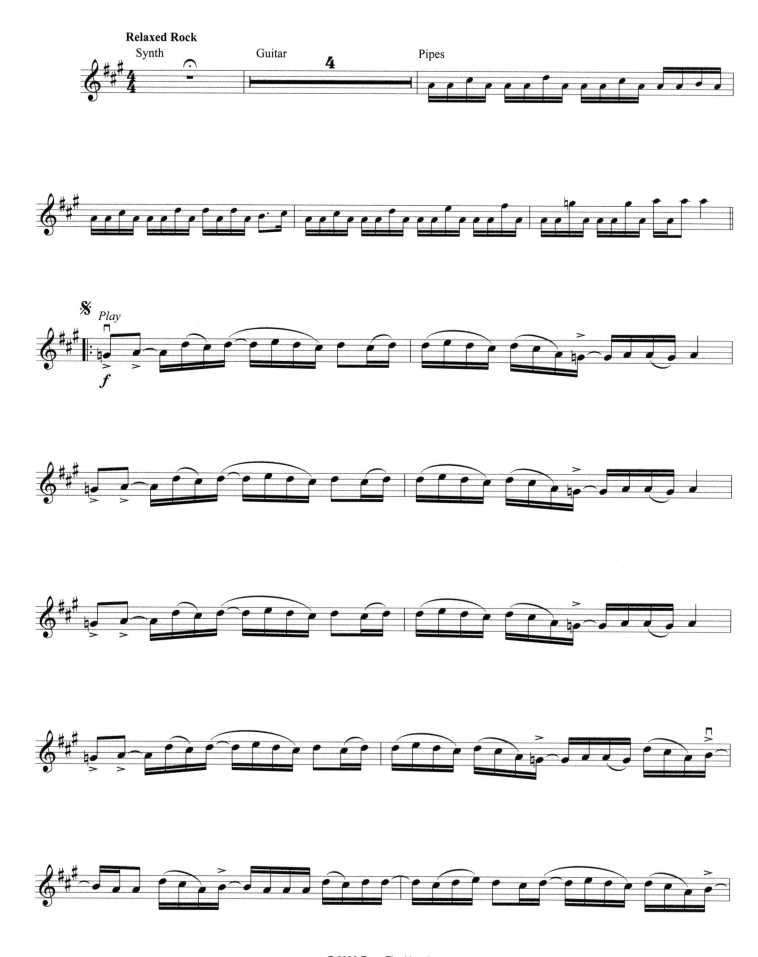

To Coda ⊕

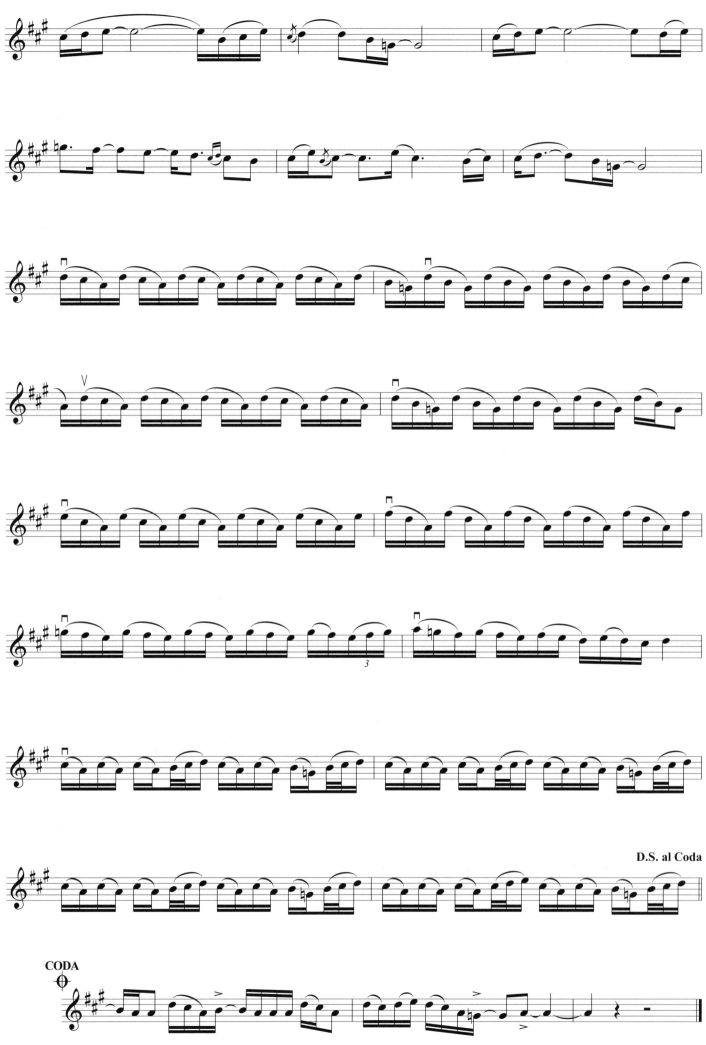

D.S. al Coda

CODA

Preacher on a Pony
(The Right Reverend Brother Guilderness' Jig/The Langstern Pony)
Traditional
Arranged by Boiled In Lead

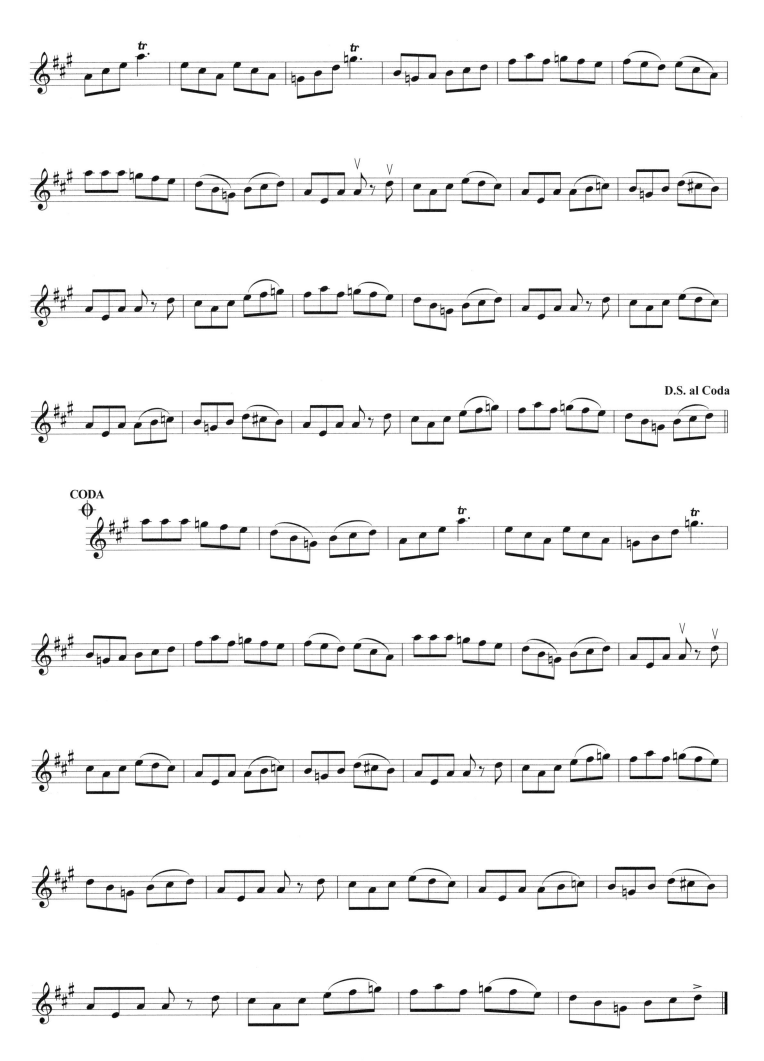

D.S. al Coda

CODA

U.S.A.

**Words and Music by Anthony Broderick, Aaron Duggins,
Anthony Duggins, Rebecca Manthe, Peter Muschong and Michael Pawula**